MATTERS OF FACT

CATS & CAT LOVERS

OTHER MATTERS OF FACT BOOKS

MATTERS OF FACT

CATS &
CAT LOVERS

ANN HORNADAY

AN IRENA CHALMERS BOOK

Longmeadow Press

**PREPARED FOR LONGMEADOW PRESS BY
IRENA CHALMERS BOOKS, INC.**

MANAGING EDITOR: **Carlotta Kerwin**
ASSISTANT TO THE EDITOR: **David Chestnut**
COPY EDITOR: **Linda Stern**
PICTURE EDITOR: **Lisa Sorensen**

———————

COVER DESIGN: **Karen Skelton**
ART DIRECTION AND DESIGN: **Helene Berinsky**

TYPESETTING: **Pica Graphics, Monsey, New York**

———————

CONTENTS

PICTURE CREDITS

p. 8 Illustration by Oscar Berger   10, 36, 39, 58 Culver Pictures,
Inc.   19 Burton Berinsky   26 The Library of Congress Picture
Collection   40–41 Cartoon by McHugh/Wilen   42–43 Cartoon
by Mort Gerberg

PICTURE CONSULTANT: ILENE CHERNA BELLOVIN

CATS INSIDE & OUT

Cats. Watchful. All-knowing. They glide silently into the night carrying their secrets with them. They seem to be wrapped in mystery, but physiology has an explanation for everything.

ZZZZ . . .

Cats are the sleepiest of mammals—all those naps add up to around 16 hours of snoozing a day.

STRE-E-E-TCH

How do cats arch their backs so high? Their spines contain nearly 60 vertebrae (compared to about 34 in humans), and the bones fit together loosely, giving them that singular, cat-like flexibility.

NO BONES ABOUT IT

Next time the cat sneaks through an opening that you *know* is smaller than she is, remember: the cat has little or no collarbone—and its chest cavity is small for its size and . . . scrunchable.

ON YOUR MARK

C. Day Lewis called it the "frantic tarantella;" whatever you call that mad racing from one end of the room to the other, when your cat is at full tilt it can reach about 31 miles per hour. (Cheetahs, the fastest land animal, hit their stride around 70 miles per hour.)

G'DAY, MATE

Big cats occur on every continent but Antarctica—and Australia. Still, the Aussies have a semimythical big cat, similar to the Loch Ness monster. The Queensland lion is supposedly tawny and rather similar to the puma, and (surprise) it has a pouch. Although some lucky walkabouts have seen the Queensland lion, it has never been captured or killed.

AGAINST THE CLAW

Why cats get stuck in trees: their claws are constructed perfectly for climbing up, and impossibly for climbing down—they curve the wrong way.

"The English cat mews, the Indian cat myaus, the Chinese cat says mio, the Arab cat naoua, and the Egyptian cat mau [and the cat's] mew is spelled in thirty-one different ways, five examples being maeow, me-ow, mieaou, mouw, and murr-raow!"

IDA MELLEN
The Science and the Mystery of the Cat

ROUGH STUFF

The cat's raspy tongue is not there to tickle the cat's owners; it is actually a holdover from when cats needed to keep a low profile in the wild. The papillae, which make the feline tongue abrasive, are designed to let the cat give itself an extra-deep cleaning, so it leaves no odor to warn off potential prey.

ENOUGH TO MAKE ANYONE
A VEGETARIAN

More plants to have on hand for the cat: Thyme, sage, parsley, lavender, chickweed, lawn grass, violets, patchouli, and cereals such as wheat or oats. And don't forget papyrus, the time-old favorite worthy of *any* feline godhead.

PLEASED TO MEET YOU

The cat lover Anitra Frazier, in *The Natural Cat*, suggests the following protocol when meeting a feline for the first time: "First, put your hands behind your back and, bending over, reach out to your cat with just your nose. Then stop, be still, and wait. This approach to a cat—this overture with the nose— demonstrates great trust and friendliness, because you are exposing your eyes and face without having any defense in reserve."

JUST A NIP

If you are out of catnip, just reach to the spice rack for some valerian, an herb known to bring on the same ecstasy as the real thing.

UP TO SCRATCH

Cats do not scratch trees in order to sharpen their claws. They are tearing off the ragged edges of the sheaths of their talons, which they shed regularly throughout the year.

NO-FAULT PREDICTIONS

For a while, the U.S. Geological Survey had a federal budget for tracking animal behavior—including that of cats—to see if animals could predict earthquakes. The U.S.G.S. took its cue from the Chinese, who had been using animals as quake-predictors for years. However, no statistical evidence came up to support the common claim that cats run away from home just before a quake. The animal network is no longer "on line."

JUST THE RIGHT ANGLE

"Catty-cornered"—being diagonally situated—is so-called because of the side-to-side saunter of the cat, according to Carl Van Vechten in his *The Tiger in the House.*

SPLASH

The Turkish, also called the Turkish Van, may be the only breed of cat that actually *enjoys* swimming.

EN POINTE

Cats feet are digitigrade, which means that cats get around on tip-toe—good for running. (The rest of us are plantigrades, that is, we support ourselves on the foot's bone network placed flat on the ground—good for standing around.)

NO WONDER YOU NEVER SEE A CAT HITCHHIKING

The cat does not have a thumb, but you can feel the vestiges of that finger on the inside of the leg, almost where it meets the foot. The claw—called the dew claw—is there, but the thumb bone never developed.

THOSE COOL AND LIMPID GREEN EYES

They may look eerie or magical or just plain scary, but the cat's glow-in-the-dark eyes have a physiological explanation. The *tapetum lucidum,* a membrane that coats the eyes, reflects the light. This ability to reflect light, along with extraordinary sensitivity to ultraviolet rays, enables the cat to see in the dark. Cats discriminate brightness seven times better than humans.

I wonder why the French cat is always "he," and the English cat is almost always "she," even when confessedly a Tom."

AGNES REPPLIER
The Fireside Sphinx

AND THEY DON'T TIP OVER GARBAGE CANS

Psychological experiments on the learning ability of animals place the domestic cat below monkeys but above the chick and the rat. They are probably brighter than horses—maybe even as bright as raccoons!

E-NUN-CI-ATE!

Du Pont de Nemours, the 18th-century French cat historian, made a meticulous study of cat speech and discovered that cats make not only simple vowel sounds, but also the consonants *m,n,g,h,v,* and *f*—in French, moreover!

READY TO BOUNCE

19th-century physicist John Tyndall is said to have observed that the elasticity of the cat is only one-tenth less than that of India rubber.

THE CAT'S MOIRÉ

The term "tabby," which describes a garden-variety striped or mottled cat, came from the Spanish word *tabi,* which denotes a cloth that resembles watered silk.

TAKE A PICTURE; IT LASTS LONGER

The cat is one of only a few animals that can stare fixedly into the human eye.

PURR-FECTLY BUILT

What separates the lion from the common cat? Lions cannot purr, and that's the bottom line. In 1916, a British zoologist separated cats into two groups—*Panthera,* which have an undeveloped hyoid apparatus (a series of bones at the base of the throat), include such animals as the lion, tiger, leopard, and jaguar. They are unable to purr and can only roar. *Felis,* which includes not only the tomcat but the mountain lion, have a fully developed hyoid apparatus and thus are able to purr but not roar.

MINE ONLY KNOWS "I'M HUNGRY"

Jules Champfleury, one of the earliest champions and documentarians of the cat, counted 63 variations of *meow*. ''But,'' he admitted, ''the notation of them is difficult.''

A STYLE TO WHICH
THEY'VE BECOME ACCUSTOMED

Longhair cats are said to be quieter and more docile than shorthairs, some say, because of their legacy of being luxuriously petted.

YOU CAN TAKE THE CAT
OUT OF NATURE . . .

The cat's standoffishness is not due to some inherent feline snobbery. It is just that cats have been domesticated for only 5,000 years, compared to 50,000 for dogs. They still have one paw in the wild.

GOOD ANTENNAE!

Cats' whiskers are extremely sensitive: a blind-folded cat was able to put his front paws on a table top when only his whiskers had touched its edge.

MAYBE WE SHOULD LET
THE CAT DRIVE

Yet another reason for the feline air of superiority: cats do not get carsick, unlike dogs and people. No one knows quite why, but maybe it has something to do with the inner ear. Balance, after all, *is* everything.

Estimating in units of caresses, as it were, the power that could be accumulated along a cat's back, an engineer calculated that at least nine thousand million strokes would be necessary to light a seventy-five watt bulb for a single minute.

FERNAND MERY
Her Majesty the Cat

SIXTH SENSE

Cats have a sense, between taste and smell, that is thought to communicate to the brain's sexual centers. Its conductor, the Jacobson's organ, is located in the roof of the cat's mouth. When the Jacobson's organ is in action, the cat opens its mouth slightly and wrinkles its nose. This response, called the "flehmen reaction," is thought to bring the chemicals of some particularly stimulating odors in contact with the Jacobson's organ.

SHAKIN' ALL OVER

Why does the slightest brush of a hair produce a shudder all through the cat's body? Cats have little raised areas all over the skin that react to the lightest touch. Called tylotrich pads, or touch spots, they send a split-second response through the nervous system and produce that singularly feline frisson.

CURRENT AFFAIRS

The old tale that a cat passing her paw over her ear signals a storm may have a basis in scientific fact. It could be that cats are trying to massage away the annoying effects of waves of electricity that go through them when a storm is building up.

HAIR OF THE . . . CAT?

A pregnant or birthing cat has been known to gratefully accept a wee glass of sherry—purely for medicinal purposes, of course.

MY, WHAT BIG EYES . . .

Cats have the greatest eye volume in proportion to body weight of all mammals.

CHAMPAGNE TASTE ON A HALF-AND-HALF BUDGET

Cats have a penchant for nitrogenous fermentation. That's why those little pink noses are so turned on by the smell of soda water, fresh plaster, ammonia—and the sweat of their owner's brows.

CHEMICAL REACTION

When your cat goes crazy over catnip, he or she is actually responding to the chemical nepetalactone, which is almost identical to an essence excreted by the female cat. Maybe that is why it's toms that love catnip the most.

Cats are rather delicate creatures and they are subject to a good many different ailments, but I never heard of one who suffered from insomnia.

JOSEPH WOOD KRUTCH
The Twelve Seasons

I THOUGHT THEY WERE CONTACTS

A white cat with one blue iris and one yellow may *look* a little cockeyed, but the two-toned look may be a Darwinian protection against deafness, which is congenital in blue-eyed white cats.

BIGFOOT

Polydactylism—exemplified in the six-toed cat—is especially prevalent in seaports, because the anomaly may have been introduced to the United States by ship's cats. Perhaps six toes improved their sea legs on those slippery decks. (PS: double-toed cats bring good luck.)

BUT CAN THEY SWAT AT BUTTERFLIES

The cat, the giraffe, and the camel are the only animals that walk by moving the front and hind legs first on one side, then the other.

If you would know what a cat is thinking about, you must hold its paw in your hand for a long time.

JULES CHAMPFLEURY

NO THANKS, I'M ON A DIET

Ever wonder why you cannot bribe your cat with a cookie, but sweets *will* do the trick for a dog? Simple: cats do not have sweet receptors on their taste buds.

WANTED: OWNER WITH PLENTY OF TLC

The ragdoll cat may be the strangest breed ever. Bred from a mother who had been injured in an accident, the ragdoll hangs limp in ones arms like a beanbag and is virtually helpless in the world.

I CAN SEE CLEARLY NOW

Cats' faces are flat between the eyes, so their two eyes work together—a rarity in the animal world. Their stereoscopic vision allows them to judge distances, focus more acutely, and see three-dimensionally.

MY MOTHER, THE CAT

Cats are terrific adoptive parents and have been used in zoos and breeding farms to jump into the breach if the natural parents cannot be there. Cats have even been known to lovingly rear a litter of mice and rats while continuing to hunt the rodent cousins in the wild. Some other orphans cats have fostered: silver foxes, martens, squirrels, skunks, hedgehogs, pigs, and timber wolf cubs.

CLEARED FOR LANDING

That useless-looking pad midway up the cat's foreleg *does* have a purpose: called the carpal pad, it is supposed to be antiskidding insurance for those rare crash landings.

NEXT TIME YOU FIND YOURSELF TRYING TO BURP THE CAT . . .

According to experts using sonograms—and accounting for differences in size—the call of a kitten and that of a baby are identical.

TWO'S COMPANY, BUT THREE'S A CLOWDER

No, a cat clowder is not something you eat with oyster crackers. A group of cats is called a clowder; a litter of kittens is a kendle.

CHAPTER 2

MAKING CAT HISTORY

Since they were domesticated 5,000 years ago, cats have witnessed history, attended triumphs and tragedies, and slept at the right hand of kings and councillors.

CLASSY ROOTS

The Egyptian goddess Bast, symbolized by the cat, was the giver of bountiful harvests, fertility, and happiness. For this reason, cats were revered in ancient Egypt. If a house was on fire, the cat was saved first.

T.G.I.F.

The Norse goddess Freya was the patroness of fertility and happiness and was closely identified with cats: her chariot was drawn by two of them. Friday, named after her, became a sacred wedding day in northern Europe. During the 15th century, when the Pope stopped pagan worship, Friday became the black Sabbath.

LONG MAY THEY WAVE

The term *ailurophobe*—one who fears cats—comes from Herodotus, the fifth-century B.C. Greek historian, who called the cats he met in Egypt *ailuroi*: ''tail wavers.''

SIBLING RIVALRY

When the Greek god Apollo created the lion to scare his twin sister Diana, the goddess of the moon brought her brother down to size by bringing the *lion* down to size—she created the cat.

FIRST THE BAD NEWS . . .

The cat-o'-nine-tails was invented in ancient Egypt, where the first nine-lashed whip was fashioned out of the skins of sacred cats. The victim of its lashings was also its intended beneficiary: a flogging with the cat-o'-nine-tails was meant to impart the cat's strength and intelligence to the luckless errant.

FAITHFUL ARTICHOKE DEFENDER

The word "cat" first came into popular use during the 4th century. Palladius recommended the *cattus* for protection of artichoke gardens against vermin.

FELINE INSPIRATION

Cleopatra's elaborate eyeliner was probably inspired by the eyes and facial markings of her cat.

JUST ASK DOCTORS

St. Yves, the patron saint of lawyers, was often accompanied by, or even drawn as, a cat to symbolize all of the evil qualities associated with lawyers.

HARD-HAT CAT

When engineers building the Grand Coulee Dam ran into some trouble threading a cable through a pipe, they came up with a limber solution. They tied a rope to the cable, then a string to the rope, then the string to the tail of a cat, who expertly crawled through the labyrinthine pipeline, successfully finishing the job!

ALLIED CATS

A British officer in Burma during World War II thought up an ingenious way to get the Burmese to support the Allies against the Japanese. He painted cats on army vehicles and kept white cats on base at his army camp. The Burmese, who valued cats very highly, believed that the sacred spirits must be with the British and went promptly to the side of the angels.

Maybe he got the idea from the ancient Persians, who hit on the strategy of strapping cats to their shields when they stormed an Egyptian fortress. The Egyptian forces could not offend the all-powerful cat goddess Bast and were forced to lay down their arms.

ET TU, FELIS?

In some paintings of the Last Supper, you will spy a cat sitting at Judas's feet.

BETTER PLEAD
TEMPORARY INSANITY

Because cats kept vermin away from the grain and food stores, it is no surprise that they were well loved in farming communities throughout history. In 10th-century Wales, they were especially revered, and there was a whole body of jurisprudence covering their worth. A cat murderer who was tried and found guilty had to pay the owner either a sheep (with lamb) or enough corn to cover the cat when its lifeless body was hung by the tail and its nose just grazed the floor.

COMMUNITY PROPERTY

According to the same law, if a husband and wife separated, he got the cat.

IMPERIAL FELINE

The 10th-century Japanese Emperor Ichigo was fascinated with cats, which had recently been imported from China. The story goes that on the 19th day of the ninth month of the year 999, a litter of kittens was born in the palace. He ordered a staff of royal attendants to see that the cats were properly fed and clothed; he even named one cat Myobo no Omoto, or "lady in waiting." She was the fifth lady of the court.

EEK, A CAT

The Glenturret Distillery Ltd. in Scotland claims to have employed the greatest mouser on record. Towser, a tortoiseshell, averaged three mice a day, racking up 28,899 kills by her death in 1987.

BY ANY OTHER NAME

Just as we call all male cats Tom, in 16th-century Britain they were called Gilbert, abbreviated to Gib or Gyb. The term *gib cat* has come to signify an old male who has seen better years.

TRES MAGNIFIQUE!

The French breed of blue shorthair, the Chartreux, is said to have originated at a Carthusian monastery, bred by the same monks who invented the liqueur Chartreuse.

THE BAD OLD DAYS

Cats were used as target practice in pre-Elizabethan England. Archers would hang them from trees in bags or leather firkins (casks) and fire away.

INS AND OUTS

After their pariah status during Europe's Dark Ages, cats finally returned to favor, especially in France, where in the 17th century it was de rigueur in every country house to cut a *chatière,* a little opening in the door for the cat's easy commerce.

GUTTERSNIPE

The smallest domestic cat is the Singapura, which averages between 4 and 6 pounds. Singapuras are also called drain cats, because they prowl the drain system of their native Singapore.

STAR TREATMENT

For one brief and twinkling moment in 18th-century France, cats had their place in the heavens with the rest of the astronomical menagerie. The astronomer Joseph Jérôme de Lalande took a little here from the star formation Hydra and a little there from Antlia Pneumatica and made the constellation Felis. Although Felis is still on the books at the Paris Observatory, eventually its stars were returned to its more well-known progenitors.

BECAUSE IT WAS THERE

A four-month-old kitten climbed the Matterhorn—14,690 feet—in the Swiss Alps on September 6, 1950.

YOU SOLD THEM FOR *WHAT*?

It was in 1890 that 180,000 mummified sacred Egyptian cats were auctioned for fertilizer in Liverpool. One ton of what today would be priceless antiquities went for about three pounds sterling.

WORKING GUY

The British Museum was kept rat-free for 20 years by Mike, a cat that maintained punctual and loyal service from 1909 to 1929.

WAR EFFORTS

During World War I, 500,000 cats were drafted by the British Army to give soldiers early warning of gas attacks.

UNCLE SAM WANTS *YOU*!

In 1948, the United States embarked on a Cats-for-Europe campaign to save the stores of food being sent overseas from decimation by rats. Paperwork and visas were expedited, exit permits hastily issued, and thousands of heroic American alley cats were rounded up and flown to the embattled war zone.

CLOSE CALL

In 1949, Illinois bird lovers successfully propelled a leash law for cats through the state legislature. However, Governor Adlai Stevenson vetoed the bill, concluding, "The problem of cat versus bird is as old as time. If we attempt to resolve it by legislation, who knows but what we may be called upon to take sides as well in the age-old problems of dog versus cat, bird versus bird, or even bird versus worm."

MERCI, DOCTEUR

One of the cat's unwitting champions during the 19th century was Louis Pasteur, whose work in hygiene gave Europeans pause about their pets. The heretofore beloved dog was now touched only with white gloves, whereas the meticulous cat was seen as the paragon of cleanliness.

FAME IS FLEETING

At the Metropolitan Museum of Art in 1987, thermoluminescent dating revealed that the famous 300 B.C. bronze Egyptian cat—a favorite of museum-goers and a hot pinup subject—was not what it appeared to be. The statue was indeed made of bronze but not of any material available to artisans of that period. The cat was quietly removed from the Egyptian gallery and sits in not-quite-our-dynasty limbo, that is, Met cold storage.

EXTENDED FAMILY

Dusty, a cat from Bonham, Texas, gets the award for most prolific mom: she gave birth to her 420th kitten on June 12, 1952.

FELINE ARCHIVE

The largest collection of cat literature is in the Glendale Public Library in California. It houses over 20,000 items on cats, from cat art to cat zodiac signs.

LONG OF TOOTH

The oldest cat on record was Puss, owned by Mrs. T. Holway of Devon, England. The old Gyb turned 36 on November 28, 1939, and died the next day.

A RUM-TUM MONEY MAKER

The musical *Cats*, which is based on the poetry of T.S. Eliot, has enjoyed a Broadway run of seven years and has grossed $133 million.

Gather kittens while you may;
Time brings only sorrow;
And the kittens of today
Will be old cats tomorrow.

OLIVER HERFORD

FAMOUS CAT PEOPLE

Cat lovers are a breed of people. The objects of their affection are devoted companions: witty, graceful, and always ready to dine, to play, and to rest between naps.

WEARING HIS HEART
ON HIS SLEEVE

Mohammed was well known for his dedication to his cat, Muezza. So dedicated was he that he once cut off a sleeve of a robe rather than disturb Muezza, who was sleeping on it.

PAVLOV WAS RIGHT

As Charles Dickens was reading one night, his candle went out. He lit it, petted his cat, and went back to his book. Shortly thereafter, the light flickered again. There was the cat, snuffing out the candle with her paw and waiting to be stroked.

HOLIER THAN MEOW

Mark Twain, a famed ailurophile, named some of his favorites Blatherskite, Sour Mash, Stray Kit, Satan, and Sin. His daughter once said, "The difference between Papa and Mamma is that Mamma loves morals and Papa loves cats."

ZING!

Brahms was decidedly *not* a cat person. He would often sit at his window trying to hit cats on the street with a bow and arrow.

BUNDLE FOR BRITAIN

During World War II, a British Government Minister went to visit Winston Churchill, who was recovering from the flu. Churchill's cat, Nelson, was curled up at the foot of the Prime Minister's bed. "That cat is doing more for the war effort than you are!" Churchill reportedly said. "He acts as a hot-water bottle and saves us fuel and power!"

I love cats because I love my home, and little by little they become its visible soul. A kind of active silence emanates from these furry beasts who appear deaf to orders, to appeals, to reproaches, and who move in a completely royal authority through the network of our acts, retaining only those that intrigue or comfort them.

JEAN COCTEAU

GOOD ANSWER

When asked by a radio host what he would take to a desert island with him, Christopher Milne (a.k.a. Christopher Robin of *Winnie-the-Pooh* fame) replied that he would take a pregnant cat.

BACKSEAT WRITER

When the great American novelist Henry James wrote, a cat often sat on his shoulder.

CARTOON CRITTER

Jim Davis, creator of the comic-strip cat Garfield, does not own a cat. His wife is allergic.

WHITE HOUSE CATS

The first White House cat came even before the White House: Martha Washington kept cats at Mount Vernon and even installed a special door for them.

Theodore Roosevelt was a great cat lover. He recounted to his children how Tom Quartz, the White House cat, wrapped up a late-night policy session the President had had with the Speaker of the House. "He spied Mr. Cannon going down the stairs, jumped to the conclusion that he was a playmate escaping, and raced after him, suddenly grasping him by the leg. Then loosening his hold, he tore downstairs ahead of Mr. Cannon, who eyed him with iron calm and not one particle of surprise."

The first Siamese cat was introduced to the United States as a gift to President Rutherford B. Hayes.

VIOLIN CONCERT BY PROFESSOR TOMKATTINI

THE CAT STAYED HOME
TO READ THE REVIEWS

The only film of herself that Ethel Barrymore went to see was *Night Song,* in which she co-starred with her cat.

Cats can be very funny, and have the oddest ways of showing they're glad to see you. Rudimac always peed in our shoes.

W.H. AUDEN

OF LUCK AND BLACK CATS

King Charles I of England was convinced that his black cat brought him luck and carried the pet everywhere. When the cat died, Charles reportedly cried that his luck was gone; the next day, he was arrested and later beheaded.

HOLD EVERYTHING

Abraham Lincoln once momentarily halted the Civil War when he found three orphaned kittens in General Grant's camp. He took them under his coat and saw that they received proper care and feeding.

"It all started when my neighbor became allergic to Punkin

DO NOT DISTURB

Albert Schweitzer, who was awarded the Nobel Peace Prize in 1952, became ambidextrous in deference to his cat, Sizi, who would habitually fall asleep on his left arm. The left-handed doctor would continue to write prescriptions with his right hand, keeping his left arm motionless for Sizi's comfort.

UNCOMMISSIONED WORK

Scarlatti's *Cat's Fugue* is said to have been cowritten by the Italian composer's cat, who daintily picked out the composition's theme as she walked up the keyboard.

here, and asked me to look after her."

NOVEL ADVICE

When asked by an aspiring writer his advice on how best to conduct a writerly life, the novelist and critic Aldous Huxley replied, "My young friend, if you want to be a psychological novelist and write about human beings, the best thing you can do is to keep a pair of cats."

THE CAT AND THE SONGBIRD

The Swedish soprano Jenny Lind was discovered as a young girl, when an alert passerby recognized her gift as she sang to her cat in a window seat.

AILUROPHILE . . .
AND AN AILUROPHOBE

Said Boswell of Samuel Johnson: "I never shall forget the indulgence with which he treated Hodge, his cat; for whom he himself used to go out and buy oysters, lest the servants, having that trouble, should take a dislike to the poor creature."

He goes on to say, "I am, unluckily, one of those who have an antipathy to a cat, so that I am uneasy when in the room with one; and I own, I frequently suffered a good deal from the presence of this same Hodge." Anything for art.

TRAILBLAZER

The first female ever admitted to the Artists' and Writers' Club in New York City was Minnie, a stray midtown cat. Minnie was a notorious card-game kibitzer, and a great favorite of Caruso's. The famous Italian tenor would stroke her as he sipped his martini.

BUT AT NIGHT, HE DREAMT OF LIONS

Ernest Hemingway's wife Mary built a special "ivory tower" for Hemingway to write in—and to house the 30 cats that roamed their household. The cats kept mostly to the ground floor, except for a few of Hemingway's favorites, who were allowed atelier privileges: Crazy Christian, Friendless' Brother, and Ecstasy.

I call my kittens "Shall" and "Will" because no one can tell them apart.

CHRISTOPHER MORLEY

BON AMI

The French author Collete wrote of her beloved cat: "She has the modesty that belongs to perfect lovers, and their dread of too insistent contacts. I shall not say much more about her. All the rest is silence, faithfulness, impacts of soul, the shadow of an azure shape on the blue paper that receives everything I write, the silent passage of paws silvered with moisture."

They say the test of [literary power] is whether a man can write an inscription. I say, "Can he name a kitten?" And by this test I am condemned, for I cannot.

SAMUEL BUTLER

NOT BAD FOR NUMBER TWO

When Petrarch died, his beloved cat—the poet's chief companion during his later years—was put down, embalmed, and buried in a niche decorated with marble and a Latin inscription declaring the cat to have been 'second only to Laura,' Petrarch's human heart's desire.

BON MOTS

In an effort to help a friend who had to get rid of his cat, humorist Dorothy Parker quipped, "Have you tried curiosity?"

Wanted by a lady of rank, for adequate re-muneration, a few well-behaved and re-spectably dressed children to amuse a cat, in delicate health, two or three hours a day.

Advertisement in a German
Newspaper

CHAPTER 4

CATS IN LEGEND AND LORE

Sacred and profane. Here are some intriguing tales and legends of cats and their ever-changing status from demigod to demimonde devil.

WHITHER THE MANX'S TAIL?

The Manx lost its tail when the cat was late for the Ark and Noah shut a door on it.

Another story says that the original Manxes (which were actually brought to the Isle of Man by galleons from the Far East in the 16th century) maneuvered around the slippery rocks on the island by slipping and sliding on their behinds, eventually erasing any traces of a tail.

Irish invaders of the Isle are held to blame in another legend. It seems the soldiers took kittens' tails to use as plumes for their helmets.

WEATHER CATS

In Scotland and Japan, tortoiseshell cats are thought to predict storms.

In the Ozarks, a cat lying curled with its head and stomach up is a harbinger of bad weather; if it yawns and stretches, clear weather is ahead.

When a cat scratches a table leg in Scotland, to this day, it raises a gale of wind.

When storm clouds gathered in medieval eastern Europe, people quickly let the cat out of the house, to avoid being hit by lightning. Cats were thought to be possessed by the Devil during thunderstorms, and lightning bolts were hurled from on high to exorcise the evil spirits the cats embodied.

In an Indonesian rain ritual to restore parched earth, a cat used to be carried around a dry field three times, then dipped in water. If the cat used was a black one, all the better to darken the sky with rain clouds.

PLEASE SIR, MORE

According to Islamic lore, cats close their eyes while they drink so that if Allah asks them if they have had their milk, they can honestly answer they have not seen any and receive a second saucer.

GOOD PUPILS

The Chinese custom of telling time by a cat's eyes comes from the traditional and astute observation that their pupils dilate and contract according to the sun's strength.

BATTEN DOWN THE HATCHES

In England, cats were used as harbingers of floods. When the cat jumped up on a shelf or a beam, high water was on its way.

RINGING APPROVAL

The kink that is sometimes seen in the tail of the Siamese cat was put there long ago when a Siamese princess bathed in a pool. Taking off her rings, she slipped them onto the tail of her cat, which then bent its tail to keep the rings from falling off.

MIDNIGHT SNACK

The Hindus say that a cat seeing moonbeams reflected in a bowl of water will lap at them, believing them to be milk.

AND TWICE AS BIG AS HER STOMACH

The eyes of a hungry cat will dilate up to five times their normal size when the cat sees its plate—even if the plate is empty.

BIENVENU

Medieval French peasants christened their "house cats" with a special ritual: "Whoever would keep his cat at home without straying has to take the cat and carry it three times round the pot-hanger and then rub its paws against the wall of the chimney, and if it is properly done, the cat will never leave."

COLD NOSE, WARM HEART

The Chinese believe that during the summer solstice, June 21 (the longest day of the year), the cat's usually cold nose stays warm all day.

AWAY IN THE MANGER

According to an Italian legend, a cat gave birth in the stable at Bethlehem at the same moment as Mary.

WELCOME HOME

The Russians believe that a cat moving in ensures happiness in a new home. According to another superstition, you should throw the cat on the bed first thing. If the cat begins washing itself, it will stay.

GRAVE MATTERS

When a member of Siamese royalty died, before he could be properly buried, he would be interred with his cat in a special chamber outfitted with holes. If the cat escaped, that meant that the prince's soul had safely entered the animal, and the prince was duly buried in a temple, with honors.

BUENA SERA

A Roman passing one of that city's 140,000 cats may nod for good luck.

ANCIENT RELIEF SYSTEMS

Some Japanese place a black cat on the stomach of someone suffering from spasms.

WOOPS!

The ancient Celts believed that if you accidentally stepped on the tail of a cat, a serpent would sting you.

GET THEE BEHIND ME

In the Lorraine region of France during the 19th century, a black cat may well have been a witch in disguise. If you crossed paths with a particularly ferocious black feline, you were advised to make a fork sign with your fingers. If the cat turned out to be a witch, you'd be hex-proof.

FOLLOW THAT CAT!

According to French legend, you can find buried treasure if you tether a black cat at the spot where five roads meet, let it go, and follow it.

TO THE SEA IN SHIPS

All ship's cats are said to be called Minnie.

Three bad omens on a ship: a pregnant woman, a clergyman, and a black cat.

A cat frisking on deck portends a gale.

Sailors call the small ripples that sometimes appear on an otherwise calm sea by the name cats' paws, because they are said to be caused by the ghosts of ship's cats dancing ahead of a squall.

FRINGE BENEFITS

Chinese proverb: A light-colored cat will bring its owner silver; a dark-colored cat will bring its owner gold.

NEIGH-SAYERS

Medieval French peasants believed that if a cat was in a cart and the wind ruffled its fur at the same time it passed over the horses, then the horses would tire forthwith. If any part of an equestrian's clothing was made of cat skin, his horse would carry double weight.

WHY THE CAT STOLE THE ANCHOVIES *AND* THE ICE CREAM

An Arab belief held that when a woman gave birth to twins, the one born last, called the *baracy,* would be prone to insatiable cravings for certain foods throughout life and would often take on the shape of a cat to satisfy these cravings.

NO CATS, PLEASE

If a cat jumps over a coffin that has a body in it, the dead person's soul is in danger unless the cat is killed immediately.

RUMOR MONGER

If a neighbor's cat comes calling, it means that the cat's owner is talking about you and that the cat will take back more grist for the gossip mill.

Kiss the black cat,
An' 'twill make ye fat;
Kiss the white one,
'Twill make ye lean.

ENGLISH COUNTRY RHYME

BLUE BLOODS GONE BAD

Some say that the Maine coon cat was bred when Marie Antoinette, hearing the tumbrils' approach, sent her cherished cats over to the United States to escape the Revolution. When they arrived, they turned feral, mating with raccoons and breeding the big ring-tailed domestic cat we know today.

THIS WON'T HURT A BIT

In Brittany, if you pull the lone white hair from a black cat's tail without getting scratched and keep it carefully, it will bring you good luck.

TAKE THAT!

One Christian myth has it that God made the cat to one-up the Devil, who had just created the mouse.

DON'T GO, PLEASE STAY

To make a wandering cat stay close to home, butter her paws.

ILL OMEN

If a tortoiseshell climbs a tree in Normandy, an accidental death is at hand.

THE MUCH MALIGNED MAY CAT

In Sussex, a cat born in the month of May will not be a good mouser but will instead attract snakes, lizards, and other reptiles.

SCAT!

In China, cats were believed to have the power to bring back the dead; thus cats were kept away from unburied bodies.

MYSTERY DATE

Some Chinese also believe that when a cat washes its face, a stranger is about to visit.

ALLEY-OOP

Next time your cat is cleaning under its tail, grasp the outstretched leg and make a wish. (Easier said than done.)

I *KNEW* YOU WERE GOING TO TELL ME TO GO PLAY WITH THE CAT

The eyes of a black cat mixed with the gall of a man was a charm for second sight in Britain. Opting for less drastic measures, many an English mummy would encourage her children to play with a tortoiseshell to achieve the same effect.

BUT THEY STILL HATE BANANAS

The first cat was born of a lion and a monkey—and from the latter cats got their playfulness.

HIGH SIGN

The Japanese bobtail, traced in that country over centuries, owns a short, curled tail like a rabbit's. When seated, the Japanese bobtail will often raise one front paw, a sure sign of good luck to come.

MORE ALBACORE, PUSS?

A Welsh superstition indicates that feeding your cat well makes for sun on your wedding day.

WATCH WHERE YOU STEP

A French girl who accidentally steps on a cat's tail will take one more year to find a husband, but a girl from the Ozarks who does the same thing will be married within the year.

BLESS YOU!

If a cat sneezes in front of the bride on her wedding day, hers will be a happy marriage.

AGE BEFORE BEAUTY

According to European folklore, a cat at age 20 turns into a witch and a witch at 100 turns back into a cat.

GLAD TIDINGS

Giving your sweetheart a black kitten will bring luck.
But under no circumstances give her a dog.

WISHFUL THINKING

When you see a one-eyed cat, make a wish, spit on
your thumb, and stamp your thumb into the palm of
your hand. Your wish will come true.

ETIQUETTE LESSON

Why cats eat and wash afterward: a cat caught a
mouse and was preparing its repast when Mouse
admonished Cat for its bad manners—dining without first washing its face and hands. Mortified Cat
dropped Mouse and began its ablutions. The quarry
promptly ran away. Ever since, cats have washed
up *after* dinner.

INGRATE!

According to the Japanese, a dog will remember a three days' kindness for three years, while a cat will forget a three years' kindness in three days.

There was a young curate of Kew,
Who kept a Tom cat in a pew;
*   He taught it to speak*
*   Alphabetical Greek,*
But it never got further than μ.

Said the curate, "Dear Pussy, you know,
Is that really as far as you go?
*   If you only would try,*
*   You might get up to π,*
Or even ν or ρ."

ANONYMOUS

FELINES AND FEMALES, UNITE!

"He who has a cat for his friend will certainly marry an immoral woman," according to an old proverb.

HERE'S YOUR HAT, WHAT'S YOUR HURRY?

While it may be good luck for a black cat to visit your house, if he stays, watch out. And carry any stray cat into your home at your peril.

AH-CHOO!

Pliny recorded this Arab legend of the cat's creation: "The rats had increased so fast in the Ark that they were eating up all the animal food, regardless of others. Noah decided to get rid of them, and seeing the lion nearby, gave him a pair of bellows. The lion, taken aback, sneezed, and out of the sneeze there sprang a cat, the very first to wage war on the rats."

CAT TALES

Cinderella started out as Cinders-Cat in the original Italian folktale, in which the heroine, a humble and overworked stepdaughter, lives on the kitchen hearth. As the story traveled to different countries, the cat's role evolved—from the girl's wearing of a cat skin as she sat by the fire, to the prince's arrival in the guise of a cat, to the fairy godmother's taking the shape of a cat. By the time the story became "Cinderella," any trace of Cinders-Cat had disappeared.

WHAT'S YOUR MANTRA?

According to Sally Ellyson, Hatha Yoga—a system of yoga consisting of a series of stretches and breathing exercises designed to bring higher awareness to its practitioners—was invented by a cat. When a young Indian prince was learning to meditate, he was having trouble concentrating. As he watched a cat stretch herself, arch her back, spread her toes and yawn, he learned some of the basic postures of Hatha Yoga and, imitating the cat's purr, began to recite the now-familiar *Om.*

MOST HONORABLE CAT

In Japan, a cat with a black patch on its back is called a kimono cat and is thought to be a vessel for the souls of ancestors. Kimono cats are often sent to live in sacred temples.

WELL-BREAD

In 19th-century Anjou, France, if a cat entered a bakery while the dough was being put in baskets to rise, the dough would not bake properly and the loaves would be of inferior quality.

OF CATS AND MAMMON

In Lyons, France, if cats aren't good for bread, at least they're good for dough. In *The Cat and Man,* Gillette Grighle tells us that a black cat is lucky *if* it bears a little white tuft in the coat. And if you find a piece of its dung in your snoe, you'll soon be coming into money. Or you could meet Fairy Gouttière, a strange cat that provides endless riches to those lucky enough to please him. In Lorraine, someone who makes a quick buck is said to "have a black cat."

POINTS OF REFERENCE

BOOKS

Antique Cats.
  Katherine McClinton. Charles Scribner's Sons.
The Archetypal Cat.
  Patricia Dale-Green. Spring Publications Inc.
The Basic Book of the Cat.
  William Carr. Charles Scribner's Sons.
The Book of the Cat.
  Michael Wright and Sally Walters, eds. Summit Books.
The Care and Handling of Cats.
  Doris Bryant. Ives, Washburn Inc.
Caring for Your Cat.
  Howard Loxton. David & Charles Inc.
The Cat.
  St. George Mivart. John Murray.
The Cat: A Complete, Authoritative Compendium of Information About Domestic Cats.
  Muriel Beadle. Simon & Shuster Inc.
The Cat and Man.
  Gillette Grighle. GP Putnam's Sons.
Cat Catalogue: The Ultimate Cat Book.
  Judy Fireman. Workman Publishing Company Inc.
The Cat in the Mysteries of Religion and Magic.
  M.O. Howey. Castle Books Inc.
The Cat, Past and Present.
  Jules Champfleury. George Bell and Sons.
Cat Scan.
  Robert Byrne and Teresa Skelton. Atheneum Publishers
Cats.
  Eleanor Booth Simmons. Whittlesey House.

Cats and Cats.
    Frances Clarke. Macmillan Publishing Company.
The Cat's Pajamas.
    Eleanor Fleischer. Harper & Row, Publishers Inc.
Centuries of Cats.
    Claudia deLys. Silvermine Publishers.
Champion Cats of the World.
    Catherine Ing and Grace Pond. St. Martin's Press Inc.
A Clowder of Cats.
    W.S. Scott. John Westhouse.
Doris Bryant's Cat Book.
    Doris Bryant. Ives, Washburn, Inc.
The Fireside Sphinx.
    Agnes Reppelier. Houghton, Mifflin Co.
Guinness Book of World Records.
    Alan Russell, ed. Sterling Publishing Co. Inc.
Her Majesty the Cat.
    Fernand Mery. Criterion Books.
In Celebration of Cats.
    Elizabeth Hamilton. David & Charles Inc.
The International Thesaurus of Quotations.
    Thomas Tripp. Thomas Y. Crowell Company.
The Lion Sneezed.
    Maria Leach. Thomas Y. Crowell Company.
The Little, Brown Book of Anecdotes.
    Clifton Fadiman. Little, Brown & Co. Inc.
The Modern Cat.
    Georgina Gates. Macmillan Publishing Co.
Moncrif's Cats.
    Francois-Augustin Paradis Moncrif. The Golden Cockerel
    Press.
Nine Lives: The Folklore of Cats.
    Katherine Briggs. Routledge & Kegan Paul Inc.
A Practical Cat Book.
    Ida Mellen. Charles Scribner's Sons.
The Science and the Mystery of the Cat.
    Ida Mellen. Charles Scribner's Sons.
The Tiger in the House.
    Carl Van Vechten. Alfred A. Knopf Inc.
20,000 Quips and Quotes.
    Evan Esar. Doubleday & Co.
The Ultimate Cat Catalogue.
    Lesley Sussman and Sally Bordwell. McGraw-Hill Inc.
You and Your Cat.
    David Taylor. Alfred A. Knopf Inc.